SINNERS DANCE

Library and Archives Canada Cataloguing in Publication

Epp, Darrell, 1972-, author
    Sinners dance / Darrell Epp.

Poems.
Issued in print and electronic formats.
ISBN 978-1-77161-285-2 (softcover).--ISBN 978-1-77161-287-6 (PDF).--
ISBN 978-1-77161-286-9 (HTML)

    I. Title.

PS8559.P72S56 2017   C811'.6   C2017-906762-1
                                                   C2017-906763-X

Published by Mosaic Press, Oakville, Ontario, Canada, 2018.

MOSAIC PRESS, Publishers

Copyright © 2018 Darrell Epp

Printed and Bound in Canada

Cover art and interior illustration by Gord Pullar

Design by Courtney Blok

ONTARIO ARTS COUNCIL
CONSEIL DES ARTS DE L'ONTARIO
an Ontario government agency
un organisme du gouvernement de l'Ontario

We acknowledge the Ontario Arts Council
for their support of our publishing program
We acknowledge the Ontario Media Development Corporation
for their support of our publishing program

Funded by the   Financé par le
Government   gouvernement
of Canada   du Canada

MOSAIC PRESS
1252 Speers Road, Units 1 & 2
Oakville, Ontario L6L 5N9
phone: (905) 825-2130

info@mosaic-press.com

www.mosaic-press.ca

SINNERS DANCE

DARRELL EPP

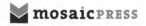
mosaicPRESS

Other works by

Imaginary Maps (Signature Editions, 2009)

After Hours (Mosaic Press, 2016)

Contents

"…and I only am escaped alone to tell thee."   --Job 2:15

Balloon, Balloon

and guess what? i did see her again, years later,
holding hands with a fire-breathing carny,
skipping through burlington's royal arboretum.
no, it was an imposter, an understudy in a wig.
i choked up thinking about the unreliability of

the senses, the pathos of the stars in the eyes
of movie extras, waiting for their big break.
my mind's a grey balloon: rinsed in a cloud,
ensnared by a maple branch, popped, done,
wondering who to give her old records to.

at least the rage is gone. the imposter flips
her hair like rita hayworth. the carny flexes
his muscles. i wish i'd brought my camera.
that's then. now, ikea parts lie on the floor.
i'm pretending i know how to assemble them.

Trick Of The Light

saw the man in the moon in a macchiato latte.
dreamed of saying one true thing but couldn't
quite pull it off, skating by the black hole's lip
and putting our files in alphabetical order is as
close as we get. saw the devil and his double
in the faces of the riders of the king west bus.
saw two co-workers laughing, patching up
their differences at the retirement party with
the open bar and the fried wontons, salvation
is like that, traveling incognito or doling itself
out in dribs and drabs. saw a child screaming
because the halloween store was sold out of
superman costumes, told him 'superman's a
jerk, he made lois lane wait 75 years for a
marriage proposal, what do you call that?'
did his mother thank me for my words of
consolation? no she did not. saw silverfish,
saw ants. saw spiders spinning frantically
under the stairs, their industry, their cold
murderous ambition, was baffling. old lp's
and hockey skates: i saw them too. saw
stars dancing, converging, forming new
constellations, it was just an illusion but
still an opium-like peace flooded my mind.

Ultimatum

looking out the soul's bloodshot window
the tintinabulations of the bells
break my heart like old yeller,
the family dog whose time had come.
it's epiphany sunday. it's st. patrick's,
they're the only bells left since the
presbyterians sold out to the hipster
condo kings. bronze queen victoria
smiles out at the royal connaught,
named after her third son and in
a state of transition. join the club.
dog-paddling in the swamp between
rush of cause and clang of effect,
i call the sun's corona a crown,
everything should have a chance
to be royalty, everything should
burst into fruit, then flame, then
fertilizer. out past the spires,
elephants on stilts, earthquakes
a la carte, solar systems reduced
to math problems for the foreign
exchange students. this brain really
doesn't match those drapes.
one of us will have to go.

High Wire Act

i was having a hard time dealing with change.
inventing new words, secret syllables and
diphthongs, was a sort of way of coping.

rebel angels disguised as outdoor cats
followed me around. i chose my words
carefully, avoided unlucky numbers.

i read the psalms, the tabloids, tried my
hand as an escape artist. wizards from
9 countries entrusted their locks to me!

lily's parents were good circus folk, we'd
wake in the dark, throw knives at each
other, dance on a thread without a net.

where do you see yourself in five years?
i tried not to laugh. recalcitrant dreams
held me fast. the cats licked their lips.

finally I ran out of jokes and card tricks.
grow up, she said, and take the tap-
dancing gorilla with you when you go.

On the Occasion Of Losing One's Guiding Light

the desire to change, to molt,
to sprout wings, to morph into
mythology puffs out my chest,
stiffens my spine, but i get so
distracted by j-lo's divorce and
a remake of a remake that now
it's time for bed and i haven't
even shaved. ochre creeps along
the maples before their leaves
irrevocably fall into the gutters.
halloween trees look so naked
it's hard not to laugh, or cry; it
depends. in grade ten science
class, lisa double-dared me to
stick my tongue down her throat.
endoplasmic reticulum, seminal
vesicles and what's the difference
between mitosis and meiosis?
she had a thing for athletes. i
saw her at the dollarama, her
kids were alarmingly savage.
she was pale, paler as i stared
until she become translucent
as a jellyfish. the space station
that crashed into tamil nadu,
i'd been using it as a sort of
homing beacon. now it takes
twice as long to walk home.
i'll trade you a stale-dated
manuscript and a sympathetic
smile for just one gold trophy.
it doesn't have to be solid gold.
gold-plating or just a few strips
of gold paint will do. you can
even pick the sport, i'm easy.

Third Eye

and the wrong words make you listen. there's
nothing left to blame the parents for. i rub my
forehead raw, wishing the key still worked at
our old apartment, i'd go back and tidy things
up, see what the new occupants have done to
the place. i check my reflection, there's light
shining out of my skull, wrapped in silvery
tissue like a christmas fruit. how embarrassing.
i find a hat, slouch it low like a noir detective.
out on the street i can hear the thoughts of my
fellow citizens, they're nothing worth hearing.
dracula thumbs a ride, says the well's gone dry,
and if he notices the hole in my head he plays
it real cool, one has to in his line of work.
mad max the road warrior asks me directions.
i shrug out an apology, i know where he wants
to go but can't explain it, it's a sense memory
like playing scales, you can't just tell someone
how to ride a bike, or how to evade a bounty
hunter by throwing yourself out the window
without cutting yourself on the glass, hoping
you remember how to roll, hoping the horse
is still where you left it, no, there's no words
for that, you just hold your breath and go.

Words Of Wisdom

nelson said 'never go to bed with someone who has
more problems than you do.' I found this advice
oddly energizing; it set the bar pretty low for me.
nelson's energized by vain dreams of moving to
hollywood. i told him 'get on with it,' same thing
i told gerald with his sandstone sculptures of
playboy playmates and former disney starlets.
he used to carve faces into tree trunks, it made
him so happy it made you happy just thinking
about it, like we were happy subletting a mouldy
basement, snorting speed with homer simpson
and savouring the drip, staving off the future
with corny jokes and the idiotic testosterone
of youth. transfixed like ecstatic monks we
watched the sun crash behind the royal bank,
watched the boston ivy race up the brickwork.
when a hailstorm broke through the heat wave
we fell silent, the whole world felt like church
and when lightning flashed in horizontal
sheets it almost explained everything.

Sweet Enough

alien abductions are on the rise,
according to the new york times.
what's more, ufo's change lanes

without signaling. the earth has
other problems as well: tourists
kidnapped in distant deserts, my

broken shoelace. i stare at your
high school yearbook photo and
wait for it to reveal its secrets. i'm

thinking of a baby bird, thrashing
its way out of the egg. morning will
come, count on it. tomorrow's sun

will astonish and change us like a
raymond chandler simile, sweet
enough to make the whole world cry.

Crushed Volvo

because of the traffic fatality by the 410/QEW split
because of beethoven immolating his very life for
music he'd never hear i put the record on as soon
as i got home and started kissing every discrete
object in the place. i kissed the wonder woman
and superman action figures, pretended they were
us and you were saying, 'remember that time when
i saved you from the flame-creatures of saturn.' of
course i remember all the times you saved my life,
only last week you ran your fingers down my arm
in the middle of transformers part four just before
the explosions started. the realness of that gesture
changed the world's pinions, straightened out the
wobble in our elliptical swing around the sun.
and so i kiss the wall, the vinyl flooring, knives
and forks because i'm alive and someone else
is not. speed kills. airbags can only do so much.
everything is glittering, spinning, i need a way
back to metropolis where superheroes can be
trusted to prevent tragedies, bend the laws of
time and space with a wink and a smile, wave
hello at the frail earthlings, their sandcastle
cities, their tiny flags flapping in the wind.

Elegy For Ash

we all remember act two scene three, when
she stopped laughing at his jokes. we all
saw the gerber baby turn into america's
most wanted. that kid from home alone
turned out so weird, it's hard not to turn
our kitchen utensils into deadly weapons.
what happened to cute, what happened to
vhs. i saw a guy on lottridge refuse to go
when the light turned green, he stood his
ground until they tasered him. i saw a
scream rise up in a man whose jaw was
wired shut but the scream would not be
denied, a new mouth opened up for it at
the back of his neck, its teeth were like
jigsaw blades, its tongue was lecherous.
my mentor's notebooks were full of magic
spells and lurid sigils. i said i'd be back
before dark but the chain snapped and i
had to drag my bike all the way home.
before we sprouted hairs in ticklish
places life was an infinite ramp—
what happened to our monogrammed
mittens, the interstellar empires
we built from blocks of lego?

Cover Letter

outsourced, offshored, downsized—they
replaced me with 30 cm of coaxial cable!
skills: various. extensive work history.
clerk. crying towel. cloud watcher. pro
wimp. quisling witch turned witchfinder
general. double-double-double-agent.
hindenburg wing man. ben-hur extra.
cave man/cave painter, cartwright.
bone-rolling shaman, telecommuter.
fiancé, until my rage got in the way.
liontamer, until the govt. shut down
the freak show and all the fun tiptoed
out the back door. i quit being a rodeo
clown when i looked in the mirror and
saw a soldier, deserted the army when
i saw armadas of neon parallelograms
invade the night sky, then it was mad
scientist in an alien invasion movie, no
a-list stars but a lot of familiar faces.
zagreb doubled for new york. the rest
was all green screen, the nerds with
their light pens. i've been called a team
player. i've been shot with an air gun.
hard to believe air could hurt so much
but important things are often invisible,
it takes training and grace to see them;
i think every good employee should
know this. autobiography is a sub-
genre of fiction. glass is a liquid.
light pours in, washes me clean.
when i was a gardener i couldn't
tell the flowers from the weeds.
i still tried my best. references
are available upon request.

On This Date In History

even as i purge the closet of obsolete instruction
manuals, old halloween costumes and mismatched
socks the dust bunnies gather incrementally like
coral in all the corners i missed, and all the dark
corners all over town. dorothee's working late.
a shout, some nonverbal accusation, worms its
way through the brickwork. outside there's mass
production and giant wheels rolling on into the
future, empty cathedrals re-zoned for commercial
use only, bedbug infestations in koreatown and
silk sheets in millionaire's row, out past the golf
course, the world-renowned school of business.
lust and dread in living rooms too small to live in.
and that smell, smelting ore mixed with tandoori,
you can't find that anywhere else. crane my neck,
search for patterns in the clouds as they tumble
like tumbleweeds, making it up as they go along.
there's a dog, there's a face, there's just an eye,
giant and glaring, hinting at something vast
and critical. the paper of record remembers the
birthdays of kaiser wilhelm and lord nelson but
not flash gordon, not the wolf man, not dorothee
who's filling in for a nurse who went awol,
what a crime, what a travesty, what a birthday.

Blind Guardian

weeks overdue, *dick tracy on the moon*
slides down the after hours return chute
with a clunk so existential in its finality
it induces a momentary seasickness.
next door vagrants are itching to fight
over respect and the conspicuous lack
thereof, the first ontario centre used to
be copps coliseum, victor copps was
a mayor, his daughter was a deputy
prime minister, i was night janitor
at the fortress of solitude, the pay
was lousy but i had a shiny badge,
a wrist radio tuned to superman's
private frequency. pray for us:
blind guardians, tipsy watchmen
manning the walls of civilization,
hoping the barbarians are feeling
generous. and oma's low-german
word for it, a kind of peach cobbler,
and the name of the estate she left
behind, just north of the black sea,
the blissful silence she basked in
like a song dispelling all doubt,
just before we got the call.

Ready Or Not

i didn't like it when they changed spiderman's
costume. and i didn't like it when green lantern
left the justice league of america, some guys
you just can't replace. hollywood should have
given orson welles a few more second chances,
what a waste. and toronto, searching for God
in toronto was like playing hide and seek with
the invisible man. hurry on sunrise, hurry on
sundown. on ash wednesday i almost woke
up in the wrong body, twilight-zone-style.
it happened before, a neanderthal stranger
glared back at me from the puddles along
victoria street. incrementally they replaced
my friends with androids. i try reality tv:
lies taste better when they glitter. i try
reality: the wind slaps potato chip bags
against my ankles, greedy microflora
rezone my g.i. tract and still she doesn't
come back! insects under the floorboards
bide their time. child star junkies bide their
time. whiptracks of beauty slashing through
the plasma screen glare, nameless colours,
the train wreck you can't look away from.

Here There Be Dragons

...and the police cars you rode in the back of,
counting the squares in the metal mesh,
counting parking meters, the little pep
talks you gave yourself, *nothing lasts,*
when we're old we'll look back and laugh,
degenerates you had to play ball with just
for a handful of pills, and many mountains
moving, piercing the vault of heaven, in
your dreams you were an adventurer, a
pioneer mapping uncharted territories.
lakes and rivers were nameless, yours
for the claiming. dad warned you, said
you'd fall off the edge of the world
but you were fearless, relentless, the
the westinghouse plant is ruled by
owls, the lister block's revitalized
by toronto money, goth squatters
replaced with dandified developers.
the blank spots on the map are gone
but the map is not the territory. your
rage, its absence pulses like toothache,
something about pride, something
about a fire, a top secret mission
to which you were once so devoted.

Lump

how majestically i glide over grand teton national park
now that it's less a destination to be checked off an
itinerary and more an idea, an ideal, like that epic
russian novel you pretend to have read but never
found the time. I found a penny minted during
truman's presidency but I never found time. the
buck stops here, he used to say. time flies, they
used to say, and who the hell is they? i think i
saw a few of them when i went out for goat milk
and granola, their voices were cobra-like hisses,
they'd filed their teeth into fangs. what would
the city's founders say, the lairds and the barons?
i said nothing, pinned my hopes on the lavender
still keeping its colour weeks past the first frost.
again with the grand tetons, the ziggurat of ur,
starlets, their hair bobbed and weaved, playing
it straight in a 1920's slapstick comedy. the
celluloid disintegrates. only the idea remains.
if you've got some time to kill i recommend the
planet mercury: a day is longer than a year there.
its heart is a dead iron lump. days are hot, the
nights are cold. lately it's just me and the robot
probes, now inert, defunct, not even dreaming,
leave us a message at the sound of the beep.

Short Cuts

you ask my opinion of your blood-stained manuscript
because i know art and you know a guy who knows
a guy in hollywood, his idea of fun is my idea of hell,
swimming pools inches from the ocean, pacific means
peaceful in spain, another place i've never been, and
i'll never know the name of the song i heard only
once just when i most needed it, the world-weary
chanteuse, her lamentations like heavenly bells.
you'll never make it because you want it all for
free, taking short cuts, dodging, mooching, never
choosing between the horns or the halos. read
one sentence, smell the ending a mile away.
white hat kills black hat, takes a bow, but
i'm not buying it anymore, can only praise
the font, the paper's carefully woven texture.
you want things i can't give. duplicity and
sweat drip off the pages, your third-act
plot twist is older than genesis chapter 1.
curse me, cut me out of the royalties,
it's all hypothetical anyhow, like those
imaginary trees falling in silent forests.
study the classics before polishing your
oscar. and save some sympathy for the
orphan villain who never had a chance.

Women and Children First

when the cruise ship started sinking i was busy:
stamping out random forest fires, raging against
the dark, giving the finger to the f-18 hornets
on their way to the air show, spinning a web,
digging a hole, filling the spare room with
clutter just to dull the echo. dorsal fins sliced
through the surface tension like jigsaw blades
as killer sharks described figure-8's around
the lifeboats. i saw it all on the news. a family
in yemen was vaporized by a predator drone
but that wasn't on the news. since she's gone
my bed no longer smells like limes, there's
no dried flowers in my vintage paperbacks,
none of her kisses hiding in mutsu apples.
diligently i cross items off a checklist that
stretches infinitely, trip over brokeback
bonsai christmas trees and toploading vcr's,
stare at parallel lines until her face doesn't
lurk in random puddles, chase the moon
over the escarpment. still a spider lays its
eggs inside a sacrificial caterpillar and a
panhandler mixing lorazepam with wine
roars in triumph as the apocalypse
he promised finally comes to pass.

The Germans

a squirrel dodging rush hour traffic reminds me
of the dogfights in *star wars: a new hope*. dead
leaves remind us that the sun is rapidly running
out of hydrogen. you remind me of garbage day
but most things aren't just one thing all the way
through, our bodies tell one story, our shadows
tell another. one man's glacier is another man's
ice cube. weeds don't think they're weeds, they
think they're just flowers that got lost. i poked
a cloud, it echoed like a hollow stage prop, a
papier mâché replica. i thought myself into a
corner until i was just a head on a stick, a brain
in a jar, the germans have a word for it i'm sure,
present yet absent and unable to colour within
the lines, this tree with its helicoptering maple
keys provides a remedy, a sort of answer—now
it's a table, a baseball bat, once there was just
a seed on the third day of creation, dreaming
of bringing vast forests to life with just a word.

Magic Bullet

when gargling with thorns make sure
not to choke on the roses. consider
mixing it all up in a blender, like the
magic bullet they advertise on late
night infomercials. the payments
are easy, the product's endorsed by
punchy boxers and celebrity psychics.
out in the dark there's a bullet with
my name on it but it's hard to fear
when the fever is subsiding and
captain kirk is beating the gorn just
like he did when we were young,
stardate something something. spit
out the fruit, save the rinds for some
rainy day when the worms wriggle
on the sidewalk dodging predators
and high heels. for a species without
brains they do pretty well. I put my
ear to the pavement, listen close
for the grand plan that keeps it all
in line without e-bulletins or fancy
uniforms but all i hear is dorothee
saying 'don't forget the eggs, they're
on sale.' that's enough. it always is.

Art in Theory and Practice

on a day between holidays when the royal bank
won't clear your cheque but won't say why, when
you're worried about your wisdom tooth and luke
skywalker just cannot believe who his father is,

picture it all as a work of art, the sky a moirè-
patterned grid, a fresco, a mural paintstakingly
daubed on an etruscan cave wall. imagine your
downtown's a space-age bible scene, boot jets

instead of sandals, leaky brake fluid instead
of water turned into fine wine. or is monday
surrealism day, with winged tigers and a toaster
on my head? art is a foreign country where we

inhabit pain, wear pathos like armour, then lie
to the border guards and return home chastised,
alive, finally more than spectators. tell it to him,
somebody tell him, the scrap metal scavenger

on the corner, sweating, cursing it all. i reach
for a half-assed prayer by default, there's glass
between us, and if i ran out to him, how to
explain, and even if i could, what next.

A Lesson in Civics

every city needs a frankenstein! civilization
demands a scapegoat. community unity
needs an 'other', an outsider who can
unite us in a ritual act of purgation--
the tribe would fall apart without it.
we need someone besides ourselves
to blame, someone to nail to a tree,
to bear our sorrows, to cleanse us
anew when we drive him out with
pitchforks and torches. last month
we scapegoated a whole family of
frankensteins. they talked funny,
they dressed weird. their differences
reminded us of what we have in
common, the ties that bind our
tribe together. our lawns were
vandalized, our pets disappeared,
our property values were threatened.
we covered them in tar and feathers.
we marched them into a box car
heading down to galveston texas.
we danced and sang all night. our
tight-knit community, once again,
had survived. our city is a good
city with a venerable history. we
don't know what form the next
scapegoat will take but we know
every city needs a frankenstein.

On Our Way To Somewhere

you can't get there from here. i mean,
by the time you cross the finish line
you're someone else. science has
proven this. some die from the
exhaustion of becoming. never
mind being. never mind sleeping.
there's no redemption without some
suffering but i'm impatient, i fast
forward through the opening credits,
the commercials. so many new toys
it's hard to keep track. there's a sub-
molecular shiver we share with the
maples and even the rocks. are the
gaps between the stars meant to be
intimidating or inspiring? are we
acid or base? what time is it? so
what? i stood and watched as stan's
diner became a vacant lot, a 7-11,
another vacant lot, and the future
site of a glass condo tower. by then
the sun had set, metallic particulates
smudged out the stars and i needed
some help with my jigsaw puzzle.
start at the edges, work your way in.
if i had a big hammer i could force
everything into place. carrie come
back with my missing puzzle piece
and i'll forgive the phone bill, the
cable bill and the mint condition
comic books you used as coasters.

Song for William Holden

framed by an arched thermal window, a robin
pokes at my brickwork, glares, flies away.
a bug hangs off my light bulb. it's not a
spider (only four legs), its ghost-thin
appendages are long and double-jointed.
i dream of empty sidewalks, old movies,
that press conference in grand bahama,
your stoic sunglasses, that lady saying
'i never thought i'd live long enough to
see william holden shoot a woman.'
'she shot me first!' you said, as if that
would fix things but boys and girls see
things differently, we can't even agree
on what 'is' is. you cut some corners,
used cheap materials in the towering
inferno but i forgive you, i'm no better.
i made good people cry, i made bad
people money. i was selfish, now my
self is all i have. i'll take the wild bunch
over the mona lisa, a smile from dorothee
over peace on earth. i keep typing because
i like the sound, i crane my neck, stare
up at the light bulb like it's the whole
wide world before adam's great fall,
before we'd done a single thing wrong.

Song for the Atom

in the keening whirlwind of dead leaves,
thursday's skirling dirges, martin's
adderall falderal, summer's rictus
grin, birds in their quintillions
packing their bags, dredge up a
weather-beaten sort of love
for ward 3, her phosphorescent
ghosts, her bricks, her atoms
waiting for fusion. or fission.
any port in a storm. out with
a bang. no guts no glory. at
alamagordo we carved up
atoms and translated desert
sands into glass, it's called
trinitite, it's in the museum
next to the siberian meteor.
when the high fiving died
down bainbridge said to
oppenheimer, 'now we are
all sons of bitches.' atoms
hide in plain sight, bide
their time, if they ever get
organized they could run
the whole show but we're
too busy to notice: netflix,
spam, the curve of the
hip of the target cashier
as she strains to bag our
made in china whatevers.
when the leaves clog the
gutters you can hear them
whisper: new for old, black
holes for stars, unquenchable
fires, the tiniest of sparks.

Song for Chicken Little

the sky was falling. or were we just growing taller?
onward we marched, destined for greatness the
palm reader told us, and she had an honest face.

every detail was filed away in case of future
depositions: edwardian dormers, chinook
winds whipping a cloud into a double helix,

microbial species vital to the blueprint hidden
behind the curtain. the grammar of the grimoire
and spinning constellations like the chandeliers

on the titanic. and the photo we enlarged until
we saw the hand of the killer, his pistol poking
out of the hedge and still it added up to nothing,

just a mime playing tennis with air. i stared into
the mirror, wondered who'd be the first to blink.

The Width Of A Circle

...and 3 days just discussing a hole, its hypothetical
dimensions, the best deals on shovels, free trips to
zanzibar flying on nothing but air miles, whose car
should we take and how many red lights, what
if stalin hadn't dropped out of seminary,
what if elvis had never joined the army?
dandelion battalions were ready to pop
but first we had to settle this free will
vs. determinism thing, cosmological
fine tuning as ontological evidence,
and that one about the tortoise and
the hare, the rabbit couldn't catch up
because of a quirk of math according
to zeno who believed motion wasn't
possible, especially if you're lazy
and amazon celebrates pentecost with
red hot deals. spoiler alert: the turtle
cheated. jumped the gun, bribed the
judges, got jacked up on dianabol,
you name it. one good yank and the
dwarf maple came right out, dead,
rotted, drowned, improper drainage,
the mushrooms clinging to the
roots told the whole sad story.

This Much I Know

we see only a fraction of the curse we labour under.
think of an iceberg, waiting for centuries to shred
open the guts of the titanic luxury liner. kate and
leo knew the score but not me. i don't know you,
don't know myself. i know this room, the story
of the spruces out front keeping the glare off my
monitor. i know the robin, the dead raccoon in
the bike lane. a corpse so close, a *memento mori*,
and me alive, non-heroic but still grateful, life
and death like two melodies in contrapuntal
motion. I know the times, the hours, when to
run and when to bow low, when to stand still
and let it rinse over me. i taste dust in my
mouth, like my atoms were recycled from
ancient atlantis or cowboy ghost towns. the
sun vaults over the trees, over the shingles.
debunked philosophies and sand-buried
empires zip by me on tiny toy tricycles.

Outliers

maybe you don't think a squirrel dodging trucks
on the expressway signifies much of anything
in an ambitious city of steel and glass towers,
with a deepwater port and a gleaming new
train station, and knotty branches of oak,
sheathed in ice, groaning under the weight,
barely registering in the peripheral vision
of bank tellers and crown prosecutors yet
signifying something dreadful, irrevocable,
like a thread of yellow police tape all around
the block. maybe you recognize dofasco's
electric arc furnace, it melted steel into putty
and rattled my fillings loose, it's gone, silent,
i wasn't there long enough to get the buyout.
'head office' is in luxembourg, now. i found
an office job, nathan is pipefitting just south
of the arctic circle, dario's x-raying concrete
for his uncle, i don't know about the rest.
and maybe cowardice is all that keeps you
from murder when traffic snarls, camaros
rev pointlessly, panhandlers preach about
the end times and c.i.a. mind control and a
hummingbird dives like a laser-guided bullet
signifying the squirrel just ran out of luck.

What I Like Is Flight

heavy metal winds slam the monarchs
against the red brick. the red brick says

'crips 4 life.' the monarchs make do,
search for cover behind the dumpster.

i saw them once, pinned under glass,
it made me sad. what i like is flight,

those thin-as-paper wings pushing
them across the continent, the jittery

jagged flight paths, now here, then
gone and so silent, so unperturbed

by stock market corrections, north
korean missile tests. emissaries of

grace, they make you to stare until
the grudges fall from your fingers,

every monarch a machine sculpted out
of rainbow, some other butterfly's

one and only, dancing on nothing,
coaxing a smile like God in disguise,

like God playing hide and seek, then
coughing to give the game away.

On The Quantum Superposition of Clouds

i broke the law, i got scared, i ran back to the church.
but the catechism had changed while i'd been away.
turns out moses didn't look like charlton heston at all.
hell's air-conditioned. sin's in rehab in taos new mexico.

that's how it goes for me. canada geese autotune their
migratory hymns. the really lazy ones just lip-sync. last
year's health food is this year's carcinogen and bigfoot's
just a hyper-thyroid loner loser in a cheap gorilla mask.

quarks go before they come. get small enough and
uncertainty's the law. i poked your cloud with my
fishing rod and heard a fire alarm, did it again and
heard canned laughter from television's golden age.

if you're looking for a rock you can set your watch to you'll
go straight to voicemail. if you're looking for a tea and a
laugh i'm hiding in kate's dimple. this is where i will plant
my flag. this is where i'll be when God turns off the sun.

Thermodynamics

burrowing underground like bronson in the
great escape, skipping along the shingles,
swinging from steeples spider-man-style,
hovering, soaring just *a little lower than
the angels,* according to david king of
israel. saint. sinner. poet. psycho killer.
that was all back in the 90's, before
i learned the value of conservation of
energy. now i'm all about matrimonial
omelets with two kinds of cheese and
complaining about the idiots at city hall.
it's not just me, though; they really are
idiots. someone set the bar too low.
the life force i squandered on speedy
joyrides and sleep-free weeks is now
doled out like p.o.w. rations in stalag
17. that billy wilder really knew how
to tell a story. no nazis could stop
william holden, not with a smile like
that. my wife likes movies about jail
breaks, bank robberies, double-crosses.
i like the sun, eating itself just for us,
igniting next year's crop with its kisses,
licking the frost off our attic window.

Dinosaur Graveyard

strange news arrived this morning from saturn.
i was busy, worrying about money. martin's
fortune teller said no refunds. hissy slanders
at the staff meeting turned smiles into knives.

gravity went rogue, saturn's rings were gone,
so said the rumour. voyager 2 said nothing,
stuck in the dark between dying suns. hard
to get worked up over chunks of dirty ice

when the factories are silent and the worst
criminals never go to jail. the ionosphere
ground against the magnetosphere, popped
our ears, made it hard to love thy neighbor.

this town's a dinosaur graveyard, you can
see it in our eyes. in the canals of mars
something began to sprout, invisible to
all but the most powerful microscopes.

Left Lung

the fuzzy black spot on the x-ray reminded
him of a dark star which reminded him of a
movie but this was no movie, the specialist
was very sorry, *left lung* he said but meant
right lung, the image was reversed, how odd
to be alive, standing in the hub of the world's
sweaty churning in a miami dolphins jersey
not knowing what to say, where to aim. he
thought of that end-times prophet preaching
in front of jackson square: the beast rising
from the sea, the woman with MYSTERY
tattooed on her forehead. he wished he'd
listened, he wished he'd hugged him, why
hadn't he hugged him, he thought of being
a kid, racing his bike up the ramp, catching
air, defying gravity, moments so pregnant
they were building blocks for every other
moment, like fighting against rush hour
traffic, the endless *throbbing* of it all, he
headed down main west toward james st.,
he'd find that guy waving his homemade
signs, he'd touch him, and as the stock
exchange wound down, as tanks moved
across the desert, confess everything.

After The Flood

...water all around, rocking catherine's kayak,
we paddle furiously or just drift along, past
the desjardins bridge, site of the infamous
rail disaster, she hates being called cathy,
she'll slap you for it like water slaps the sand
as it reaches for the moon and never quite
reaches it, so close it hurts, the sweetness
of it all, it took me years to show you my
scar, i'm funny that way, change is hard,
gradually then suddenly, a change of
heart that snaps us bolt upright in our
chairs like when the babyface wrestler
turns heel, the look on the colonel's
face when he finds out jason bourne
didn't die in the explosion. they gave
us jobs, then changed the backgrounds
when we were too busy to notice.
special effects courtesy of industrial
light and magic. fatal riptides and
the years wasted fighting with dad,
running, finally finding him hiding
in your fog-resistant shaving mirror:
family reunion through a glass darkly.
i'd say welcome home but you never left.

Strange Tales

showed up at the funeral with balloons and
sparklers. the ceo gave 'employee of the
month' to a labour-saving algorithm built
by bangladeshi child slaves. the more
things change the more we need doctor
strange, hipster wizard with the all-seeing
eye, peeking into tomorrow and all of
hell's nine circles. can you keep a secret?
proton and neutrons are made from quarks;
the invincible iron man's really tony stark.
but secret identities are ticking time bombs,
eventually the mask and the face trade places
and all your friends are busy, battling loki
god of mischief, or galactus the world-eater.
monday you laugh when nothing's funny,
just to please the drone you deeply loathe
in the next cubicle; by friday you're worlds
away and shooting sparks from your hands.
reel it back in, it's a marathon, not a sprint,
remember that naked juggler on roller blades
singing *born to run* at the festival of friends,
you asked him to tell you his tricks and
all he'd say was practice makes perfect.

Imagine A Road

the elantra's car alarm beeps in vain. again.
waking up the neighbours, that yippy lab
that haunts the fire escape. a robotic howl
rolls down the asphalt all the way to lake
ontario. pop the hood, yank the plug out
of the sensor. curse the punk who backed
into the front end without leaving a note,
rattling some part that's too expensive to
fix. just disconnect it and forget about it.
stare down at the baffling mechanisms,
the buckled fender. imagine staring down
from a great height, above the clouds.
imagine a road, empty and clear with
bright spots up ahead. brood over plans,
napoleon-style, that melt in the pre-dawn
rumble of flatbeds hauling steel coils
to the honda plant in alliston. scan the
grocery store flyers for bargains. rub
your eyes, chase away those black
spots dancing behind your corneas,
writhing like souls hunting for a way
out. at least it's quiet now on barton
street, her feral cats and cold case
files all ablaze in pentecostal grace.

Passing On The Right

he'd been feeling guilty about the cornfields,
the way we'd choked them into submission,
buried them under a factory outlet mall—its
products were made by slaves and he still
couldn't afford to shop there. now his *check
engine soon* light blinked in mute mockery.
the warranty ran out a day before, he barked
out a laugh and his wife said, 'i know, eh?
can you imagine?' and continued her story
about her cousin's idiotic trip to hollywood.
he passed a minivan on the right, bopped
and weaved. the temp agency had sent
the wife to a tool and die shop, he hoped
it turned into something permanent, they
needed some good news, and now they
were running late. he looked to the east:
out of the dark the dawn's rosy fingers
clutched at the burlington skyline like
a beam of light peeping up from under
a snugly-hung door and the surprise,
the warmth of it, felt like absolution,
forgiveness from all offended parties.
and God, like an army of spies, battered
against the hungering meat of his heart.

Living At The Movies

in the movie based on the novelization of the play
inspired by a true story a terminator fell in love
with a zombie. or was it a predator. i forget. it
was arty, autobiographical, with soft lenses.
the violence was abstracted, at oblique angles.
the soundtrack was grating, electronic. the
killer's steps were steady, the femme fatale
told the lead to man up, emotions roiling
beneath the masks we mistook for faces.
'who's the real me?' the cyborg asked. 'and
where's my off switch, i'm so tired.' the
tension slackened by the third reel, the
obligatory car chase. the popcorn was
slick with faux butter, your dentyne
was mint. all movies run together in
a cinemascope epic, a celluloid river
trailing behind us. all stories starts to
sound the same. boy meets girl. he's
new in town. he has a dad. something's
wrong. he was there, now here, this,
now that, stuck in the past, unfree,
stars don't really shine, their glamour's
a rental, let me die in black and white.

House of Cards

barking mad pit bulls, running out
civilization's clock. flecks of vomit
in the beard of the local prophet.

crazy 8's with you and vito corleone,
14 floors above a mirror-cracked
metropolis. it's not a knighthood

or a mansion but it's not bad.
aging is about the narrowing
of possibilities. hit and run,

ace of spades. breakfast in
bed, candies on your pillow,
a diamond on your birthday

but don't hold your breath,
i'm just not that kind of guy.

Time Out

we were born. things went downhill from there.
and in dear leader's work camps it's even worse:

try loving thy neighbour through barbed wire
fencing, dig under it and the voltage can still

fry you. the dissidents asked for a donation but
how can you monetize my pity, all my giving

is local anyhow. i'm worried about mercury.
not the planet, the stuff in our drinking water,

and all those baby alligators we flushed down
the toilet, our sewers must be choking on them

by now. godzilla; dr.doom; name your poison.
don't forget the sales tax, don't forget lonely.

the tide roars, aching for the moon. i'm floating
now, caught up in the glowing glamourous undertow.

Helpful Hints

don't show off your skull collection
until after the second interview.

break the ice with laughter.
unless they're crying. unless

they're dying. bone up on that
local sports team, the hometown

gladiator wasting his youth in
the penalty box. don't mention

the moons of saturn, their tipsy
orbits and glaciers of methane.

not unless the boss does first.
even then it might be a trick, a trap.

better just shut up until you pass the 90-day
probationary period and you're in the union.

Two Letters

dorothee said she'd meet me in australia
but i thought she said austria where the
birds poop on statues of schwarzenegger
the home town boy who made good. mr.
universe, mr. governor, mr. terminator.
but no, dorothee had said australia, two
letters can make such a difference. look
at friendly vs. unfriendly. you can't
spell funeral without fun and what do
i know of australia besides koalas and
jailbirds? this happened when western
civilization was winding down. last
summers's trilobite collection was in a
glass case on the shelf by the toy soldiers.
we went from barbarism to apocalpyse
on a japanese bullet train, with no stops
in between. i slept through decline and
fall, classical and decadent, denial, grief
and rage. captain cave man, meet the
jetsons. last one out, turn off the lights.
it's such a long way to australia, austria
too, it's the end of the world and i can't
decide if this tie goes with those shoes.

Passengers

it's a long ride. the way back is even longer.
and power lines idiotically strutting by like
imperial stormtroopers (palpatine had the
power, vader had the pathos), you're late
you say, your period you mean, we're late
period, full stop, stunned, in a fog, bands
of mist cradling us like a mother's hands,
low-flying ghost clouds slapping against
the windshield. we left home in a horse-
drawn coach, upgraded to a lexus hybrid,
luxuriated in chariots of privilege. then
some nouveau riche brat stole our limo,
left us slumming in economy where not
even the peanuts are free. we could try
hitch hiking the rest of the way, that
used to be a fun way to meet people.
one lift was a stockbroker, flashing hot
tips like diamond-studded ace cards, he's
retired to aruba by now, another was a
ginseng farmer from tilsonburg, raging
about paying child support on a kid he
wasn't allowed to see, his regrets were
tattooed on his neck, folic acid you say,
and b-12, knitting the future inside you.

Down Payment Blues

the ephedrine kicks in halfway to dundurn castle.
leaves change, change some more, burst into

flame. greedy fingers tickle my back, feed me
lottario-fueled fantasies of a house on lake erie,

with a deck, a dock, facing south-south west.
i sign up for the overtime shift, i even cheat at

solitaire. there's no stone idol on my mantle
leering and demanding homage but without

drastic self-surgical measures the counterfeit
gods of me first and compound interest will

undo us all. *and it's not like I'm praying for*
the fifty million, just the half mil would be

fine, just enough to catch my breath...stop,
consider the lilies, holding back the frost

by sheer force of will, they don't work or
worry yet their glory is irrefutable, more

glorious than solomon and o how i want
to be like them, i'm ready: let's go.

Blush

looked out my window and saw egyptian pryamids,
that sphinx napoleon's grunts blew the nose off of.
stared at california redwoods until i became one,
a rookie member of the parliament of trees.
walked sideways like a crab, skipped over cracks
in the sidewalk until i became a super-villain
made of metal with an orbiting icy palace and
an anti-gravity cannon: one shot and all the
landowners would drift off into space and
i could move right in, king of the world.
those guys never liked me anyway. in the
parking lot outside the fertility clinic i saw
guys assaulted by their soul mates because
their boys weren't good swimmers, we
should have started sooner, we shouldn't
have been so selfish. the doctor asks if we'd
mind if the intern did the procedure, she
needs the practice. yes we'd mind, what
are we paying him for? blush. you see i lied
about the redwoods, just to make you pay
attention, like a child screaming about
monsters in the closet when he only wants
an extra hug, a ginger cookie with toffee inside,
and all the monsters moved out months ago.

Post-election Roundtable

why am i so aggressive at the teriyaki express
that used to be a mrs. vanelli's pizzeria when i
don't know anything about the electoral college,
don't even care, red state/blue state, elect a
monkey, a lemur from zanzibar and just watch,
i still wouldn't care, not the way i care about
that white hair i found in my beard, the crack
in the glass that lets the cold in, those great
russian writers from pushkin to gorky, what
a golden age, how did they do it? was it the
brutal winters, the potato-based alcohols? i'll
take a page of chekhov over all of *moby dick,*
maybe it was the cossacks instead of cowboys
that did the trick but i'll take uss enterprise
1701-1 over sputnik, you've got me there.
maybe i just like to stir the pot sometimes.
ever bite down on a parking meter just to
make sure you aren't dreaming? this food
court used to be a parking lot, before that
it was an orchard, i'll tell you when it's
time to calm down, *i know* they're looking
at us, at least they're awake now, paying
attention to something other than watery
wonton soup and i'd say it's about time.

My Kind Of Saint

on weekends
when my head is cleared

of bureaucratic gossip
and the earth's axis has

adjusted itself accordingly
the sun races down my street

that 3-lane 1-way commuters
treat like an expressway and

i can see all the way from
burlington to stoney creek

from the future to the past
these houses had front yards

before the expropriation
these yards were forests

throbbing with wild boar and
deer before confederation

before sir john a macdonald
kicked sir allan macnab out

of the way in the name of
progress once i saw a man

with no shoes give his
last cigarette to a man

with fancy boots just
because the man was

shaky from loneliness
and the naked love in

that gesture brought me
to my knees that's my kind

of saint one time a ghost
said to me you don't have

to be great you just have
to be here and pay attention.

Standing On Ceremony

seven different words for the same thing.
a preacher speaking of ezekiel
and the dry bones, the movements
of his hands, the sympathetic bond
between the left and the right.
codes indecipherable, comets
of blue and gold, christmas
cards thrown into the garbage.
the taste of hot lemon tea,
the visible world— a
mist, crowning a hill,
a metaphor for the spiritual
life or maybe its adversary,
so close to nothing at all.
flesh turned into smoke,
there's a new mystery
behind every pulse, your
hands don't shake as a life
is poured into cardboard
boxes. no words are said,
it's too late for that and
why am i not surprised.

Winter Dream

'talking about shopping is not really talking,'
she said, that's why she didn't answer
jill's texts anymore, that's why she blocked
her on facebook. i said, 'there's an
alternate world where i'm an mvp,
a vip, with dozens of grandkids.'
she said, 'that's cool,' and carved
obscenities with her thumb into
the frost caked on the window.
that winter the world was our
idea, our boozy chauffeur, our
hunchbacked prankmonkey
somersaulting on command.
the spell lasted until the cat
got sick, the vet's disdainful
looks made us feel like guilty
truants. she gave him the finger
as i paid the pharmacist, then
the pipes froze on us and nine
months later she was teaching
english on the island of kyoto.

It's Not That

it is now well-established that you can take one
thing apart and rebuild it someplace else. i'm
thinking of that australian guy and his replica
of noah's ark in kentucky (day passes include
lunch). i'm thinking of mount kilimanjaro,
with hemingway's dead leopard at the peak,
shrunk down into a snow globe perched atop
grandmother's fireplace. and february days
when ice covered the windows with claw
marks, and tree branches snapped under
the weight of it. later in the year, deer bit
the heads off the custom-bred roses my dad
saved up all year for, but they were too cute,
too noble, for him to think about shooting
them. it's not that we have come unstuck,
unable to tell if this is real life or a scene
in a movie we saw when we were kids.
and it's not that we're too afraid to ask
the guy in the next cubicle for help. it's
the loon interrupting the sermon, dying
for a miracle, the prayer team swarms
him, the pensioners are re-assured but
not me, not even when the clocks tick
on like nothing is wrong, nothing at all.

Free Movie

we laugh at funerals, cry at weddings,
ace all the trivia contests—by definition
this is trivial information. we tempt fate,
or not, play it safe when we should bet
the farm, examine things close-up with
the finest microscopes, there's a truth
inherent in the dance of sub-atomic
particles, it's our duty to look for it.
but now we're coming out of the
library after the free showing of *the
gold rush*, grateful to the librarians,
haunted by the sight of the tramp
decorating his cabin to impress
his guests, only to be stood up
on new year's eve, what a sick
joke, we swear to choose beauty
over cruelty, freedom instead of
slavery, charlie chaplin over darth
vader. mighty geologic forces rip
open cracks in the pavement, the
smell of veggie pakoras fills my
lungs and i'm gone, gasping, my
heart rattles against my ribs and
i'm madly in love with everyone.

Stolen Satori

you pull the batteries out of the alarm clock
and everything stops: your pulse, earth's

elliptical wobbling around the sun. all
those private disasters are in the past,

locked up in a trunk secured with two
padlocks. cold winter light meanwhile

beats the land into brilliant sheets of
riven diamond. your scars and scandals

are gone, it's diamonds to the horizon.
the beauty is light, is song, and how

human to turn mystery into music.
when the world's engine starts up

again you'll be ready for it, some final
catastrophe to wean you from the world.

Never Forget

the furnace rattles, wheezes asthmatically.
a door is opened, then double-bolted shut.
the garbage truck groans, skids on black ice.
dorothee mumbles 'toujours' in her sleep.
there's no need for an explanation.

Mute

...it got so bad his head just disappeared,
he replaced it with a flat-screen tv
from costco where it pays to buy in bulk.
he took long walks, kept careful records,
watched the weeds get a head start on
the flowers. the kids were extra-bratty
that year, reminding him of the times
he spoke harshly to cashiers he deemed
below his social station, *i'm the king of
sinners,* he thought with horror, *if only
i could fix things,* but it was all beyond
him. it was all he could do to pick litter
out of strange lawns *gratis,* to smartly
salute pedestrians, all kinds of them—
the married, the defiant, the lost. he
liked the time between lunch and rush
hour when the old veterans gathered
under the birch trees for chess games.
so many untold stories, so much wisdom.
he stared and took notes until the dark,
like the wings of the mighty cherubim,
swaddled gore park with infinite grace
and care. seagulls wailed and stabbed
at each other over a dry crust of pizza.

Heavy Gravities

the place silent movie actors go,
once they've been forgotten.
the spot where things get tweaked in
that moment between moments. that
tiny point we all orbit in unison,
i saw it, a black hole you
can fold into your wallet,
as unequivocal as snot on a plate
or a legion of mushroom clouds,
that winter we stayed up all night
and still couldn't fix things.
pushing you on a swing. your
mother, who worried about
you meeting 'a bad apple.'
the king who gave away his
crown to the salvation army.
the interstellar spaceship
that never left the garage.
a friend endlessly expounding
on the difference between good
and bad fats, the migration of
the monarch butterfly and his
dream of writing a self-help
book that really says it all.

Local News

a toddler lashes out in rage because her ice cream
melted before she could finish it, her howls
bounce off window-with-plywood-instead-
of-glass number 798, off curbs, off f-150's,
fizzle out in the face of the big rigs using
cannon street as a cross-town shortcut. tom
volunteers at the st. patrick's soup kitchen
on wednesdays but today he's collecting
holes, throwing them into his burlap sack
until he's doubled over by the weight.
burleigh the mantis-eyed preacher says
what do you think about syria? i said
you have got to be kidding me. the sun
gave magic powers to superman but not
to me. still it climbs, still i'm grateful,
the sidewalk warms up my bare feet
like the belly of the space shuttle
heating up on re-entry as it starts
to scrape against the atmosphere.
friction sure is something. that's
why we have wars, earthquakes.
burleigh says these are the last days.
the walk home keeps getting longer.

Surfing

the private eye investigated the kidnapping of the
millionaire's daughter, bound to a chair and held
for ransom. turned out there was no abduction,
she'd faked it all because she couldn't wait for
her father to die, she wanted her inheritance now,
not later. desert towns were obliterated, ancient
sumerian tablets ground into powder. a salesman
was poisoned and had to race against time to
solve his own murder. a tiny species of aphid
went extinct before we'd even discovered it.
flying robots murdered civilians on our behalf.
i remembered the great blackout of 2003, we
had to make do with reality instead of reality
tv, my landlord roasted a lamb off the balcony
and told me about life in romania before they
overthrew their tyrant; they killed him first,
held his trial a week later. vaguely i remember
life before remote control, or maybe it was
just a rumour, a bedtime story like straw
turning into gold, hate into love, your
credit is good with us, don't pay until
doomsday, blast away that unsightly
cellulite, the private eye draws his gun,
winks at the camera like he finally gets it.

I Dream Of Absent Friends

and when i awake a crow is poking at my boot,
the sidewalk is killing my back and the sun's
magnetosphere churns furiously, shoots ionized
high energy particles at us. in 8 minutes they'll
be jamming our radio transmissions and it's all
a little hard to believe, like someone had erased
that line between dreams and real life—what did
the arctic explorers do, when all was whiteness,
the sky and the land just one blank sheet with
no horizon? i should remember to ask them
sometime. stagger home and sort things out—
run aground on strange blind reefs of memory,
that's harder than it sounds. my short cut home
is blocked by a condo development—i don't
remember authorizing that! how odd it is to
be anywhere, with moments doled out like a
losing army's rations. there ought to be a law.
the details get fuzzy around the edges; the
minions cut some corners. i stand tough,
waiting for the next shot, but the weather
surprises me, a warm wind tumbling in
from lake ontario feels like a truce, it tastes
of russian sage and oxidation, i gulp it down
like a prisoner of a forgotten war, freed.

Things Fall Apart

the careening toboggan, the sheer frictionless
hill, gathering speed until you're breathless,
reminded of a world unspoiled, unfallen,
the way up was harder than the way down,
with slick patches hidden by fresh snow,
this is where you broke your leg when you
were twelve, cracked the tibia wide open,
split the ankle bone too, they put a steel rod
in so deep you don't set off alarms in airports,
things fall apart like mom's retinas, angie's
anemic platelets, or the way that comet
shrinks every time it swings around the sun.
crows stared blankly as your ankle swelled.
aunties prayed for a miracle. the principal
visited you in the hospital. the history
teacher mailed you a card. that was years
ago. the bottom of the glass leers up at you.
the clinic said sorry for the false positive but
there's no discount on out of date calendars,
no refunds for jokes nobody laughed at. you
try to ease up on the punk smartassery but
it's getting late, your ride left without you,
and the bikers at the bar may be smiling
at you but they're not your friends.

Days

...and days out of days somersaulting out
of tiny toy clown cars all the way down
to the cn rail switching yard at the end
of stuart street. only kids and freaks
remember to laugh—good citizens are
busy worrying about the new carbon
tax. the days, in pancake makeup,
pantomime out a warning but there's
too much static, and did you ever notice
how that jigsaw puzzle of the taj mahal
was more interesting with just a few
pieces missing? there's a lesson in
there somewhere. the days love
practical jokes, they nailed garlic
to the door, hung puppet effigies
of famous dictators in our windows.
they brought the flying wallendas
to town, had them dance along the
tightrope to nowhere, loaded the
past into a cannon, shot out a
fusillade of diamonds. the days
rev up until nothing ever ends:
at the speed of light there's just
one day. called forever. called now.

Stampede

saw her again at dundurn castle. by the
picnic tables. juggling. bouncing on a
unicycle. but she'd remarried by then,
moved back to fort erie, bought a house
by the river, in a neighbourhood realtors
called 'family-friendly' and 'up-and-coming.'
was it a dream? a false memory? a battery
of neurons misfiring out of sympathy?
post-amputation, post-incineration, time
revved up, slowed down, reversed.
wanting and having mix like eulogy
and lullaby, like donald trump and st.
francis, who gave until he had nothing
left but still had everything that mattered.
thoughts like these trample me underfoot,
thunder like buffalo stampeding across
texas, we went there once, or maybe
just saw a movie about it. objects of
desire are never static; even asleep
she was spinning away from me,
loping toward the western spiral
arm of the milky way galaxy, but
you can't lose what you never
had; i comfort myself with this.

Bastard

'Titano! The Monster That Time Forgot!' *Tower Of Shadows* #7,
September 1970

they phased out the penny without asking me.
and hot wings used to be 10 cents on tuesday.

child-proof re-sealable packaging baffles me
worse than rubik's cubes until hulk smash,
hulk so sorry. stooges and pogues laughing
at nothing, stealing pens from work, thumb

tacks and drill bits too, claiming imaginary
nephews as dependents, still it's not enough
against leviathan, against great behemoth
rising out of the ancient oceans of amnion,

drinking rivers dry and taking no prisoners.
blame irradiated vegetables, blame einstein
for the mutant black sheep chained up in the attic,
the bastard gargantua left out of the photo albums.

Stupendous Colossal Martian Cranium

'Monster At My Window!' *Monsters On The Prowl* # 27, August 1974

fatally unstuck and drunk on laser beams
looking for a break and the epcot future
walt disney promised us back when the
president was a four star army general
and technicolor suburban fathers had
smart answers for everything. my bionic
r.f.i.d. implant itches in a spot i just can't
scratch. a tap on the glass says it's lunch
time for my alien visitor. his limbs are
atrophied, his cortex so powerful i can
hear his thoughts inside my head as he
chows down on pet store rabbit food.
he's bent on world domination. so am
i. we just differ in our methodologies.
better keep it on the down-low,
the wife would never believe me.
how i love it when she dances until she shatters.
she sings ring of fire and i pick up the pieces.
and all the monkish vagrants giving me
the thumbs-up like they know something
i don't, they'd get under my skin but
there's no more room, i stand my ground,
wait for dorothee, wait for the martian
mother ship to call her children home.

A Figure Of Fun

'Jimmy Olsen, Freak!' *Superman's Pal Jimmy Olsen* #59, March 1962

it doesn't matter who's drawing me,
i'm always just the second banana.
freckled with slack-jawed innocence

a figure of fun perpetually cute and
helpless, unable to watch a movie or
even dress myself without help from

you-know-who. my life is the worst-
selling-comic book on the newsstand,
comedy relief sandwiched between

tales of intergalactic search and rescue.
i drink the mad scientist's formula that,
in a burst of slapstick, turns me into a

human porcupine for a day while the
kryptonian rescues the bottled city of
kandor from brainiac, the evil space

robot. how i would love to graduate,
to be an a-list superhero, or barring
that, to be left alone. he'll be here in

nanoseconds, like a numinous purple
comet, if i press the button on my
signal watch—but if he's so great,

why can't he sense our resentment
at the way his omnipotence makes
us all obsolete, our most urgent

actions superfluous? and he wasn't
even born here! he's an immigrant,
and we all bow down to him. how

do those people do it? i wish i could
fly, i wish i could step outside of
time and space. everybody knows

me, i'm jimmy olsen, all the papers
call me superman's best friend
and oh dear God how i hate him.

Fire Breathing Dragons All Along Sherman Avenue

'The Untold Story Of Red Kryptonite!' *Action Comics* #266, May
1960

its effects are random, unpredictable. hallucinations.
halitosis. hairy palms. one time I turned into a
minotaur. another time, a unicorn. sometimes
i see things that aren't there. sometimes i say a
prayer. droids and wookies lob water balloons
at my car. even the robot butler in the men's room
denies me paper towels. his accent is british,
regal. i reek of failure, the backwater colonies.
dofasco let me go. now that was a sweet job,
slinging chains in the hulls of saltwater ships.
we'd unload raw slabs, acid-wash them, run
them through the ovens until they were
malleable, then roll them into coils, ship
them off to be stamped into suv frames.
they used to employ 17 000 people; now it's
barely 3 000. and all because of a radioactive
meteor, all because of nafta, gatt, other
nefarious abbreviations. an imperial star
destroyer stole my parking spot. at least
that's how i remember it. mail boxes on
empty houses, palsied with rust after the
nouveau riche moved on and out, they scare
me more that lex luthor. and how he always
got paroled so easily, i'll never understand.

My Cubicle's Bigger Than Your Cubicle

we're all working away at something.
or at least pretending to. adjust the tint
and brightness of your toshiba monitor.
everyone's entitled to an ergonomically
friendly chair; if the armrest irritates
your sciatic nerve, tell the union rep.
know your rights. cc the regional vp.
save as a draft until you're sure, then
hit send. control-z beats liquid paper
any day. does anybody up there read
these reports at all? dividing ten by two:
is this what all those a-pluses were for?
why can't i work from home, why
can't i outsource this to my droid
in mumbai, why can't they stop
those lights from flickering?
hang in there, climb the ladder
they said. i say save it for the
rookies, the supervisors' nephews.
i climbed that ladder once before,
there was nothing up there, not
even clouds or a way down,
just vertigo, empty promises and
musical chairs without any chairs.

Blazing like Stars

starving for forgiveness i settled for a shwarma.
the cashier was cute, she smiled when she
didn't have to, the hot sauce was hot, with
real scotch bonnets but it still didn't help,
not after lying so brazenly and letting the
dandelions run wild after promising (twice!)
to yank them before they sprouted seeds
but now it's too late, the wind scooped
them up and down the lawn and i still
don't see what the big deal is. antique
furniture, i don't get that either. so your
table's old, so what? now the shwarma's
gone and the dandelions blaze like stars.
i like the dog star, i like antares, and the
pulsar inside the crab nebula sending out
a coded message for the dinosaurs. space
is vast, space is old and when stars run
out of hydrogen to burn i always feel sad.
i told ifrah we were made out of stardust.
she laughed and called me poindexter.
those distant lights are long dead; they're
also nurseries for new stars, gravity says so.
i pull a dandelion, put it behind my ear,
climb the stoop, ready to face the music.

Up the Hill

what with all this
coming/going
being/becoming
it's a wonder anything
ever gets done.

Cosmic Super-Reducer

...and the years you spend adding it up
trying to make the numbers agree even
as familiar signposts morph menacingly
like in a fun house mirror, as the spark
fades and brutal contingencies hobble
us at the knees, make us crawl, make
us small like a toy city under glass,
like the bottle city of kandor, shrunk
by the super-reducer ray of brainaic
the cosmic collector in *adventures of
superman* #242, tiny avatars smiling
and waving through the rage, tiny
stomachs still ravenous, insatiable,
searching for a bulwark against
fate's arrows, you know how it is:
bored in church, palm sunday,
sweating under stained glass,
the light exposing the cracks,
the dust clouds dancing in its
wake, the drop of blood in the
white of the eye, the scar that
aches but doesn't show, the
fatal wound your mother
said was just a little scratch.

There's Beauty Enough

the tilt of the world makes me stagger
i prowl on all fours for better traction

dawn rinses the world like a dirty dish
you cannot resist and why would you

it's too golden too pure a gift of grace
i check my garden like a feudal lord

shoo the robins off the blueberries
check the leaves for signs of blight

or caterpillars waiting for the change
butterflies are always welcome

smeared in pollen riding the wind
there's beauty enough to make the

rocks cry out i give thanks martin
said that ninety per cent of success

is just showing up the other ten
per cent well that's up to you.

Halo of Flies

i'm patrolling my turf, counting the windows without
glass, the bakeries and shoe stores turned into squats.
this is where ifrah hitched a ride on the handlebars of
my mountain bike, this is where lily informed me we
had nothing in common, she made it sound like she
was imparting the secret of the universe and i could
barely stifle a yawn. that's the fire escape where we
looked for mars the war god through your brother's
telescope, had chin-up contests off the ladder. i give
it a tug and the metal groans and shakes, oxidation
takes no prisoners. rust always wins but he doesn't
have to be so smug about it. i'll come back with a
camera, i'll record all the fading signage before
the demolition crews make way for gentrification.
i'm in the dog house because i forgot valentine's
day, my wife says i seem distracted, my head's
an empty bag, my heart's a corroded cog, my
left brain trips up my right brain like a saboteur,
i see consciousness as a halo of flies, as the
900-pound gorilla on the other end of the
seesaw. i step on a crack, say a prayer, give
thanks for the men who poured the concrete,
laid the bricks and pipes we take for granted,
recall there's grace enough for everybody.

Mummy

all those phone numbers i don't call anymore like bars
i no longer frequent, they're bankrupt or parking lots

anyhow, failed ventures like the edsel, the delorean,
like w.c. fields reading the bible 'looking for loopholes.'

shoeless kids ripping the heads off barbie dolls, absent
parents, gamblers who love to lose and those winters

we burrowed under a mountain of quilts, told stories,
made plans, you were like a fairy tale, wrapped up

like a mummy with bunny slippers on your feet,
trudging to the kettle and telling me not to worry.

All Politics Is Local

the mayor lied to me, he said he understood what
i was going through, he had been there himself,
then he raised my property tax, gave me a ticket
when i ran into the library to avoid paying late
fees on *Modern Living for Dummies Volume 3*,
martin said take it to court, never stop fighting,
i wanted to tell you about it but you were asleep
you were so cute in wonder woman pajamas and
buffalo bills toque, i wanted to tell you about the
time i fell asleep at the wheel, woke up unharmed
in a muddy field, gobsmacked by my good luck,
about arno the crackpot, pushing his shopping
cart full of broken clocks and writing a book on
the shroud of turin, 'it's authentic,' he says, 'and i
can prove it.' about jody the comic book guy, he
gave me great deals, rounding down whenever
the boss wasn't looking. that was in the 20th
century and the memory of his kindness still
astounds me. your eyelids flickered, your mouth
a perfect O. you never met the mayor, couldn't
care less about politics so maybe you wouldn't
understand, maybe you'd be mad about losing
your dream, maybe i should just pay up and
play it straight, follow the rules, decisions
decisions and all because the mayor lied to me.

Loose Ends

...and all the things i never told olivia—
that tablecloth was truly nauseating

why hide fat grainy cherrywood with
fred and barney and wilma and dino

the sounds this piano could have made
if beethoven had had eleven fingers

the gaps between us the jittery quarks
running interference at oblique angles

of tibia and femur umbrella and hand
secret codes science fiction dialects

and i lost my english/klingon dictionary
my darth maul light saber the force

is strong in guangdong provice
where light sabers are made

in the pillowcases and old tax returns
she left particles of dust but i prefer

fields to particles oceans of maybes to
a single dreadful spacetime

location those eiffel tower bookends
were a ripoff no matter what she paid for them.

Fist Becoming Hand

every time i blink i see a scene
of heartbreaking beauty: a
murder of crows gliding
above a sun-burnt cornfield
straining against the
vault of heaven

i have a past but now i know
i have a future too
it's there
waiting for me
all i have to do is
grab it.

Where The Action Is

looking out the window, saluting
the commuting armies of worker

drones, it's easy to feel like a king.
across the room queen dorothee

dreams of ancient beheadings and
dirty diapers, maybe, how should

i know? her sleeping body turns,
twists its limbs until she resembles

a skinny dark-haired swastika and
i couldn't be more impressed if it

started raining frogs. her eyelids
flicker as she enters a new dream

full of spies, guns and bloody old
testament bible stories. the world

outside is boring as an empty bag,
all the action is inside this room.

late for work? who cares!

He Was Right

Ecclesiastes 9:4

a living dog is better than a dead
lion, said wise king solomon,
who hated mondays as much

as we do. he was right about
so many things, life is what
it is, even when it's ugly.

the joints ache, the fenders
rust, and yet—
every sunrise is a baptism.

high tides and low tides
pregnant with their opposites,
melody of melted snow.

grace, like invisible feathers on your cheek.
life dreaming itself into wakefulness,
saying hello in angelic alphabets.

Born In The Back Of A Hearse

admiring the rebirth of
my favourite birch tree

its tiny baby buds
remind me of your eyes,

whoever you are.

to fly from the cocoon,

to be born in the back of a hearse
and wind up here,
in springtime,
in a room with a window,
the only prayer is
thank you.

it's all a bit absolute: the world
and the world that surrounds it,

the road from caterpillar to here,
things unsayable and irrevocable.

Gardening With You

a helical humming snakes its way up the hyssop.
transplantation is a shock: she trembles, sways.

the garden's ten thousand species work as a team.
my tongue presses against your clavicular dimple.

aphids and lepidoptera feast on the ephemeral.
between eye and world there's an alchemy--

photons are God's spies, dancing in the ultraviolet,
the infrared, saving their best for the visible world.

Interrogation Room

i'll tell you everything I know. don't worry,
this won't take very long. ten minutes tops.
then we're outta here. the sun is shining.
no, not here, here's it's night, and cold,
but the sun is shining somewhere.
somewhere the sun is shining. this chair
is solid. solid as it gets, i mean. i mean
it's made of atoms, and atoms are mainly
just nothing at all. particles in an empty
field. sorry. boy meets girl, how's that?
boy loses girl. girl comes back, but not
quite all the way. a stranger rides into
town. the son defies the father, the
seed becomes a tree, even genocidal
tyrants were cute once, go ask their
mothers. hollywood is no place for
kids. nobody's perfect. judge not, lest
ye be judged. love thy neighbour—
i kill a fly, i feel guilty for days.
once I saw a ufo. my heart was
pounding. my hands were steady.
the moon is pulling away from us
at an alarming rate. the days are
getting longer. i mean shorter.
i mean, can i go now?

Acknowledgments

Many thanks to the Ontario Arts Council and the Canada Council for their financial support. Thanks to the editors of the following magazines, where some of these poems first appeared:

Exile

Event

Hurricane Review

Hamilton Stone Review

Nashwaak Review, Wild Goose Poetry Review

Cloudbank

Rhubarb

Encore

Coe Review

Fiddlehead